APR   2014

CR

Biggest CHOKES in Sports

by
Jeff Hawkins

Published by ABDO Publishing Company, PO Box 398166, Minneapolis, MN 55439. Copyright © 2014 by Abdo Consulting Group, Inc. International copyrights reserved in all countries. No part of this book may be reproduced in any form without written permission from the publisher. SportsZone™ is a trademark and logo of ABDO Publishing Company.

Printed in the United States of America,
North Mankato, Minnesota
052013
092013

Editor: Chrös McDougall
Series Designer: Craig Hinton

Photo Credits: Ben Curtis/AP Images, cover, 1; John Swart/AP Images, 5; AP Images, 7, 15, 19, 41, 43, 53, 59; Amy Sancetta/AP Images, 11; Julie Jacobson/AP Images, 13; Kathy Willens/AP Images, 19; Bill Sikes/AP Images, 23; Beth A. Keiser/AP Images, 25; Gerry Broome/AP Images, 27; Ronald Martinez/Getty Images, 29; Rick Bowmer/AP Images, 31; Kevork Djansezian/AP Images, 35; Dave Martin/AP Images, 37; Ross Kinnaird/Allsport/Getty Images, 39; Tami Chappell/AP Images, 45; Doug Mills/AP Images, 47; Lionel Cironneau/AP Images, 49; Don Larson/AP Images, 51; Melchior DiGiacomo/Getty Images, 55; Fred Jewell/AP Images, 57

Library of Congress Control Number: 2013932587

Cataloging-in-Publication Data
Hawkins, Jeff.
 Biggest chokes in sports / Jeff Hawkins.
  p. cm. -- (Sports' biggest moments)
ISBN 978-1-61783-922-1
Includes bibliographical references and index.
1. Sports--Juvenile literature. 2. Sports--Miscellanea--Juvenile literature. I. Title.
796--dc23

                                                    2013932587

TABLE OF CONTENTS

Chapter 1

BIG BASEBALL CHOKES

Professional athletes are always expected to come through "in the clutch." They are paid high salaries to handle pressure with grace. And their die-hard fans demand they never make a mistake.

Professional athletes have the ability to maintain focus and excel physically in pressure-packed situations. It's part of what makes them special. But professional athletes are also human. And since no human is perfect, sometimes even All-Stars and top teams make untimely mistakes. It's the nature of sport and being human.

Take the 1984 Minnesota Twins, for example. The Twins needed a late-season win against the Cleveland Indians to stay in contention for an American League (AL) West title. After two and a half innings, the Twins were pounding the Indians 10–0. After nine innings, however, the Twins had suffered a major letdown and lost, 11–10.

Gary Gaetti and the Minnesota Twins fell out of playoff contention in 1984 after blowing a 10–0 lead against the Cleveland Indians.

When the Kansas City Royals won their game later that evening, the Twins were eliminated from the playoffs.

After the game, third baseman Gary Gaetti colorfully described the Twins' performance.

"It's hard to throw," Gaetti said, "with both hands around your neck."

The Billy Goat Rears Its Head

Billy Sianis purchased a tavern across the street from Chicago Stadium in 1934. Many professional hockey players stopped by the tavern when they weren't playing. Soon after buying the tavern, Sianis rescued a baby goat after it fell out of the back of a truck. Sianis nursed the goat back to health and named it Murphy. Soon Murphy became the tavern's mascot and often was used for publicity stunts.

The Cubs played the Detroit Tigers in the 1945 World Series. Before Game 4, Sianis was granted permission to march Murphy around Wrigley Field wearing a sign that read: "We Got Detroit's Goat." Sianis paid $7.20 for two tickets. One was for Murphy. However, Murphy was not entirely welcome.

By the fourth inning, security personnel told Sianis to remove the goat from the stands. Other fans were irritated by the goat's odor. An upset Sianis departed the ballpark and "cursed" the Cubs' championship chances: "Them Cubs, they ain't gonna win no more."

The Cubs invited Billy Sianis's nephew and his new billy goat to a 1984 playoff game, but it did not reverse the curse.

At the time, the Cubs were leading the AL champion Tigers two games to one. The Cubs ended up losing Game 4. They eventually lost the series in seven games.

Entering 2013, the Cubs had still not returned to the Fall Classic. Some call it the "Curse of the Billy Goat." Others call it bad luck and bad plays at the wrong times.

When most sports fans think of the biggest chokes in sports history, one team generally comes to mind: the "Lovable Losers." The Cubs have a long history of choking in the playoffs and late during the regular season. The team has failed to claim a World Series since 1908. The Cubs have had their chances, though.

In 1969, the Cubs spent 156 days atop the NL East. But the Cubs dropped 17 of the final 25 games and fell swiftly out of contention.

In 1984, the Cubs qualified for the postseason for the first time in 39 years. They started strong. Chicago opened the NL Championship Series by outscoring the San Diego Padres 17–2 in the first two games. But the Cubs could not sustain the tempo throughout the five-game series.

The Padres rallied to tie the matchup at two games apiece. In the deciding game, the Cubs held a 3–2 lead in the seventh inning. But then first baseman Leon Durham committed a costly game-tying error. The mishap allowed eventual Hall of Famer Tony Gwynn to come through with the game-winning double for San Diego. The Padres won 6–3 and advanced to the World Series.

Perhaps the hardest choke for Cubs fans was in 2003, though. That year the Cubs were five outs from the NL pennant. Most of the fans at Wrigley Field were on their feet. They were clapping, screaming, and dancing. The World Series felt so close.

The Cubs led the Florida Marlins 3–0 with one out in the eighth inning of Game 6. The Cubs appeared to have the momentum. Pitcher Mark Prior was hurling a three-hit shutout. As good as things looked for the Cubs, quickly, they soured.

Marlins outfielder Juan Pierre was on second base. Teammate Luis Castillo stepped into the batter's box. He lifted a foul fly down the left-field line. Cubs left fielder Moises Alou hustled to the edge of the playing field. He positioned himself to try to make a play.

Castillo's fly ball floated toward the stands. However, the ball looked like it could be drifting back to the field of play. A fan named Steve Bartman was seated in the front row. Several fans, including Bartman, reached for the souvenir. So did Alou. Bartman's hand deflected the ball first. It fell into the stands as a foul ball.

Alou was furious. He and his teammates immediately argued for fan interference. The umpire ruled against the motion.

After the call, the Cubs fell apart. Prior released a costly wild pitch. Shortstop Alex Gonzalez misplayed a potential inning-ending double play. Outfielder Sammy Sosa overthrew his cutoff man. All were fundamental errors that aided the Marlins as they scored eight runs during the half-inning. The Cubs once led the series 3–1. However, they dropped Game 6, and then they lost Game 7 the next night. The Marlins advanced to capture the World Series.

Changing History

It took a big man to ignite the storied Boston Red Sox-New York Yankees rivalry. A very big man, indeed. Babe Ruth was probably the biggest man of his day. Ruth was a mammoth figure with a larger-than-life personality.

Ruth started his big-league career as a pitcher with the Red Sox. However, he displayed promise as a power hitter. So Ruth transitioned into a full-time outfielder. Red Sox fans were thrilled with the prospect of a position switch. Except the fruits of the transition were not realized in Boston. Red Sox owner Harry Frazee in 1919 needed money and sold Ruth's playing rights to the Yankees.

Over the next 84 years, Ruth became baseball's home-run king with 714, the Yankees won 26 World Series, and the Red Sox won none. Even today, some Red Sox fans refuse to forget the transaction. The rivalry

Chicago Cubs outfielder Moises Alou falls to the ground below fan Steve Bartman after the fan deflected a ball during the 2003 playoffs.

fueled the AL during baseball's early years. Through the generations, the rivalry's competitiveness has continued to grow.

The late-season drama of 1978 is still a hot topic for fans. The Red Sox led the Yankees by 14 games in the AL East. The huge advantage on July 19 did not hold up. By the first week of September, the Red Sox's lead was down to four games when the Yankees came to Fenway Park. They proceeded to sweep the Red Sox in four games by a combined score of 42–9. That series became known as "The Boston Massacre." The Red Sox and Yankees finished the regular season tied for first place. A one-game tiebreaker was scheduled in Boston.

Bucky Dent ended the Red Sox's hopes of reaching the postseason. The Yankees' light-hitting shortstop slammed a game-winning home run over the "Green Monster" wall in left field at Fenway Park.

In 2004, it was time for the Yankees to take a tumble. And it started with a stolen base. It was Game 4 of the AL Championship Series (ALCS). The Yankees were on the verge of sweeping the Red Sox out of the playoffs. The Red Sox trailed by a run with no outs in the ninth inning. Boston outfielder Dave Roberts was on first. He needed to get into scoring position. He knew he had to go.

Legendary Yankees closer Mariano Rivera initially paid close attention to Roberts leading off first base. Not close enough, though. Roberts stole second base on Rivera's first pitch to batter Bill Mueller.

Rivera is known for one pitch: a cut fastball. A cutter, as it's often called, displays sharp movement while approaching home plate. Rivera's 1–1 pitch to Mueller must not have been extremely sharp. Mueller connected on a game-tying single. Slugger David Ortiz propelled the Red Sox back into the series with a game-winning homer in the 12th inning.

Rivera is known as one of baseball's all-time greatest closers. But against the Red Sox in 2004, Rivera was tagged with blown saves in Games 4 and 5. Both allowed the Red Sox to rally to victory. The Yankees

PHILLIES EXECUTE THE "PHOLD"

Baseball history is full of teams faltering down the stretch of the regular season. Some stumbles are just more dramatic than others. Even Philadelphia fans had trouble accepting the 1964 collapse. The Phillies and their fans needed a championship to celebrate. The club is one of the oldest in the major leagues, dating back to 1883. From 1919 to 1947, the Phillies finished last or second-to-last 24 times. With 12 games remaining in the 1964 season, they led the NL by 6.5 games and were beginning a home stand. The Phillies dropped seven straight at Connie Mack Stadium and then three more on the road. The 10-game losing streak soon became known as the Phillies "Phold."

eventually fell in seven games. They became the first major league team to lose a seven-game series after winning the first three. The Red Sox, meanwhile, advanced to capture their first World Series title since 1918.

Angels Continue to Fall

The current Los Angeles Angels of Anaheim changed their name after the 2004 season. Previously, they were known as the Anaheim Angels. Before that, they were the California Angels, and before that the Los Angeles Angels. No matter what they were called, the Angels for a while just couldn't get it right in the playoffs.

The Angels' first big choke came in 1982. They jumped out to a 2–0 ALCS lead over the Milwaukee Brewers. But the Angels could not protect the lead. In the deciding fifth game, the Angels led 3–2 in the seventh inning. But the Brewers loaded the bases for Cecil Cooper. The contact

California Angels infielder Doug DeCinces dives in vain for a ground ball during the 1986 playoff series against the Boston Red Sox.

hitter connected on a series-clinching, two-run single. The Brewers advanced to the World Series.

The Angels' second big choke occurred in 1986. The Angels led Boston three games to one. They were one strike from their first World Series appearance. But the Game 5 turning point for California came when closer Donnie Moore offered a forkball to Dave Henderson. The Red Sox slugger recognized the flat pitch attempt and connected on a go-ahead home run. Henderson also drove in the game-winning run in the 11th inning.

The Angels appeared rattled by the turn of events. They were outscored 18–5 combined in Games 6 and 7, and Boston won the series.

The Angels' third big choke came in 1995 and also left them short of the postseason. Heading into the final stretch of the regular season, the Angels led the AL West by 10.5 games over the Texas Rangers and 11.5 games over the Seattle Mariners. The Angels then started to fall. They suffered two nine-game losing streaks in about a month's time. They did manage to forge a tie with the Mariners at the end of the regular season. But the Angels' season ended after a 9–1 rout in a divisional tiebreaker game.

It would be another seven seasons before the franchise won its first World Series championship.

New York Mets players wait for their final game in 2007, an 8-1 loss to the Florida Marlins, to end.

Chapter 2

BIG FOOTBALL CHOKES

The 1980s was an era of over-the-top behavior. The University of Miami Hurricanes were truly the team of the times. As one of the brashest programs in college football, the Hurricanes played hard, talked big, and won big games.

Miami had won the national title in 1983. The Hurricanes entered the November 10, 1984, matchup against the University of Maryland Terrapins ranked number six in the nation. Guided by first-year coach Jimmy Johnson, the Hurricanes were still playing for a shot at consecutive national titles.

First, though, they had to get by Maryland at the historic Orange Bowl in Miami. Early in the game, that did not appear to be a problem. Miami's players trash-talked their way through a dominant first half. They

The University of Miami Hurricanes were the talk of college football after winning the 1983 national title.

raced out to a 31–0 lead. Perhaps the Hurricanes' confident play turned into overconfidence.

On the first second-half play from scrimmage, Maryland linebacker Scott Schankweiler intercepted a pass. Maryland backup quarterback Frank Reich entered the game and immediately took charge. Reich directed the team to its first points of the game. Miami's defense suddenly could not find the words to describe Reich's play. By the end of the third quarter, Reich had picked apart Miami's defense with two touchdown passes. The Hurricanes were silenced as their lead was cut to 34–21.

Maryland scored another touchdown. Later a pass deflected off Miami safety Darrell Fullington's fingers. The ball landed in the arms of Maryland receiver Greg Hill. He raced for a 68-yard touchdown. That gave Maryland a 35–34 advantage.

On the next kickoff, Miami lost a fumble on its own 5-yard line. Two plays later, Maryland's Rick Badanjek scored on a 4-yard run. Some Miami players walked off of the field in silence after choking away a 42–40 loss.

Bills Drill the Oilers Late

Houston fans simply call it "The Choke." What better way is there to describe what happened to the Houston Oilers during the second half of the 1993 National Football League (NFL) wild-card playoff game against the Buffalo Bills?

When safety Bubba McDowell returned a third-quarter interception for a touchdown, Houston's lead grew to 35–3. All the Oilers had to do,

WIDE RIGHT

Buffalo Bills kicker Scott Norwood had a reputation for his accuracy, not his range. Entering Super Bowl XXV in January 1991 against the New York Giants, Norwood was just 1-for-5 on field goals of 40 or more yards. Bills coach Marv Levy had to make a decision with eight seconds remaining in the fourth quarter. He could have Norwood attempt a 47-yard field goal. Or he could try to squeeze in one more play to get a closer attempt. Levy didn't want to risk running out of time. Norwood lined up and with the wind at his back launched a potential game-winning kick. It went wide right. The miss handed the Giants a 20–19 victory. It marked the beginning of the Bills' four-year run of Super Bowl defeats.

their coaches instructed, was play fundamental football and they would advance to the next round. Even many Bills fans left, figuring the home team had no shot. It did not help that the Bills' starting quarterback, Jim Kelly, was sidelined with injury. Or perhaps it did help, because the Bills' backup was Reich. He was the quarterback who led Maryland back from 31–0 to beat the nationally ranked Miami Hurricanes in college.

Reich led Buffalo to a touchdown. No big deal. Houston still led 35–10. The Oilers did not seem to have their focus on the ensuing kickoff. Buffalo kicker Steve Christie recovered his own onside kick. Things began to unravel for Houston after that.

The Oilers' defense could not stop the backup quarterback. Reich led his team down the field for another touchdown, cutting the lead to 35–17. The momentum was shifting.

The Oilers' secondary had displayed solid coverage in the first half. Now Houston could not keep Reich from hitting his top receivers,

Andre Reed and Don Beebe. Reed caught three second-half touchdown passes and Beebe caught one. Buffalo briefly took a 38–35 lead before Houston tied it 38–38. The game headed into overtime.

The Oilers caught a break when they won the overtime coin toss. But their mojo was gone. Quarterback Warren Moon threw an interception on the opening possession. The turnover set up Reich to lead the Bills down field and within field goal range. Many players on the Oilers' bench turned away as Christie nailed the 32-yard field goal for a 41–38 Buffalo win. Christie's kick also sealed the largest collapse in NFL history.

"River City Relay" Drowns

New Orleans Saints kicker John Carney just stood there, his hands glued to his hips. He could only stare toward the ground.

"NOOOO! He missed the extra point wide right!" Saints play-by-play announcer Jim Henderson screamed into the microphone on December 21, 2003. "How could he do that?"

ONE BAD MISS

Tight end Jackie Smith developed his skills as a receiver and punishing blocker during his time with the St. Louis Cardinals from 1963 to 1977. He finished his Hall of Fame career with 480 catches—and one terrible miss in his last game as a member of the Dallas Cowboys. It was the third quarter of Super Bowl XIII. Smith stood alone in the end zone. He waited for the pass from quarterback Roger Staubach to arrive. When it did, the ball slid through Smith's grasp. Stunned, he fell back in disbelief. The Cowboys settled for a field goal and dropped the Super Bowl to the Pittsburgh Steelers, 35–31.

It was as if everyone at Alltel Stadium in Jacksonville was thinking the same thing. How could Carney do that just moments after the Saints pulled off the "River City Relay," one of the most bizarre touchdowns in NFL history?

The play developed with no time remaining. The Jacksonville Jaguars were leading 20–13. On the final play of regulation, Saints quarterback Aaron Brooks completed a pass to wide receiver Donte Stallworth. He dodged several defenders before pitching to a teammate. Michael Lewis caught the ball and ran to the Jaguars' 21-yard line. He pitched to Jerome Pathon, who followed Brooks's blocking into the end zone. Unbelievable!

TAKING A KNEE

The 1998 Minnesota Vikings had a historically good offense. They led the Atlanta Falcons 20–7 in the second quarter of their 1998 conference championship game. What could go wrong? Everything. Atlanta closed the lead to 20–13. But kicker Gary Anderson had a chance to hand the Vikings a 10-point lead with around two minutes remaining in the fourth quarter. He had not missed a field goal all season. But he missed the 38-yard attempt. The Falcons soon tied the score at 27. Then on a third-down play with approximately 30 seconds remaining, Vikings coach Dennis Green called for a kneel-down play to let the clock run out and send the game to overtime. Fans wanted the 15-win Vikings to take a chance. Green wanted to play it safe. Falcons kicker Morten Andersen hit a 38-yarder in overtime to clinch the "Take A Knee Game."

The Saints still trailed 20–19. They needed a win to keep their playoff hopes alive. Carney lined up for an extra-point attempt to tie the game. He pulled it wide right. With the loss, the Saints fell out of the playoff race.

Vikings kicker Gary Anderson watches as his field goal attempt sails wide right in the 1998 conference title game.

Chapter 3

BIG BASKETBALL CHOKES

The final buzzer sounded and the players looked confused. Number two seeds are not supposed to lose to number 15 seeds in the National Collegiate Athletic Association (NCAA) men's basketball tournament. Number two seeds are powerhouses. Number 15 seeds are usually small schools or teams who barely got in. They have no business beating the powerhouses. But that is what happened—twice—in 2012.

The heavily favored University of Missouri Tigers lost to the Norfolk State University Spartans 86–84 on March 16. Then the Duke University Blue Devils fell to the Lehigh University Mountain Hawks later that day.

In 2013, Florida Gulf Coast University became only the seventh 15-seed to earn a first-round upset when the Eagles beat Georgetown University. It was the fifth consecutive tournament appearance for Georgetown in which the Hoyas lost to a team with a double-digit seed.

Duke's Andre Dawkins (20) can only watch as Lehigh's Gabe Knutson dunks during their 2012 NCAA Tournament meeting.

Follow the Fundamentals

Many modern basketball players crave highlight-reel slam dunks and high-arching, long-range jump shots. As such, many of these players overlook the fundamentals. Free-throw shooting certainly is one missing element. Another is ball security.

The Louisiana State University (LSU) Tigers proved how vital it is for a team to always maintain focus on fundamentals on February 15, 1994. By being careless with turnovers and failing to hit free throws, LSU lost a 31-point, second-half lead in a stunning 99–95 defeat to the University of Kentucky Wildcats. The outcome remains one of the most dramatic in-game collapses in college basketball history.

LSU held a 16-point lead at halftime. The Tigers continued to dominate after the break. Early in the second half, they scored 18 consecutive points to take a 68–37 lead. The Tigers were competing

NO EASY BUCKETS

All the University of Memphis Tigers had to do was hit some free throws. The Tigers had five free throws late in the 2008 men's college basketball national championship. Four times they missed. Meanwhile, the University of Kansas Jayhawks rallied from a nine-point deficit with 2:12 remaining in the second half. The Jayhawks came back by doing what the Tigers struggled to do—make a shot. The Jayhawks continued to send their opponents to the free-throw line. The Tigers continued to miss. Kansas guard Mario Chalmers's three-pointer with 2.1 seconds to go sent the game into overtime. Memphis gave up the first six points in the extra session and fell 75–68.

Memphis' Derrick Rose shoots a free throw with 10.8 seconds left in regulation against Kansas in the 2008 national title game.

at a high level in all phases of their game plan. Suddenly, LSU's tempo changed. Kentucky scored 24 of the next 28 points. LSU committed careless turnovers and missed 11 free throws in the final 12 minutes.

With 6:25 remaining, the Tigers' defense failed to contain Walter McCarty. His steal under the basket and dunk cut the Tigers' lead to single-digits, 82–74. With 1:40 to go and still leading 95-93, LSU had a chance to slow down an offensive possession and fundamentally run down the clock. That did not happen. Instead, the Tigers turned the ball over and gave Kentucky another chance.

With 19 seconds remaining, McCarty hit a three-point jumper, giving the Wildcats the lead for good. Taking advantage of the Tigers' loose defense, the Wildcats connected on 11 three-pointers over the final 15:34.

"I can't believe it," Kentucky Coach Rick Pitino said. "I know I've never, ever witnessed anything like it."

Nick the Brick

Clank.

Clank.

Clank.

Clank.

And just like that, Nick Anderson and the Orlando Magic allowed the momentum of the 1995 National Basketball Association (NBA) Finals to clang off the rim.

Nick Anderson, *right*, of the Orlando Magic battles with the Houston Rockets' Clyde Drexler during the 1995 NBA Finals.

The host Magic held a three-point lead over the Houston Rockets with 10.5 seconds remaining. Anderson had four chances from the free-throw line to put Game 1 out of reach. Four times, he missed.

The blown opportunities came back to haunt the Magic when Rockets guard Kenny Smith connected on an off-balance, double-pumping, high-arching three-pointer. Smith's acrobatic effort capped a 20-point comeback and sent the series opener into overtime.

From there, Hakeem Olajuwon leaped into NBA Finals lore. The Rockets' center connected on a buzzer-beating, tap-in field goal to clinch a 120–118 victory. The Magic failed to recover. They dropped the series in four games. The Rockets cruised to consecutive NBA titles.

During the regular season, Anderson hit 70.4 percent of his free throws. After the series, Anderson earned an unflattering nickname: "Nick the Brick."

THUNDER CRASHES

The 2010–11 Oklahoma City Thunder were led by the NBA's youngest scoring champion, Kevin Durant. However, Durant and the Thunder could not seem to score toward the end of the Western Conference finals. Oklahoma City surrendered a 15-point, fourth-quarter lead in Game 4 against the Dallas Mavericks. Dallas went on to win the NBA title.

"What can you do?" he asked years later. "I'm always going to be associated with those four free throws."

Trail Blazers off the Mark

Thirteen straight missed shots. Thirteen. That is a lot of missed shots. It is how many straight shots the Portland Trail Blazers missed in their epic choke in the 2000 NBA playoffs.

First, however, it appeared that the Los Angeles Lakers would be the chokers in the 2000 Western Conference finals. The Lakers featured guard Kobe Bryant and center Shaquille O'Neal. Many favored Los Angeles to win its first NBA title in 12 years. That philosophy was strengthened when the Lakers jumped out to a 3–1 series advantage. But the Trail Blazers briefly silenced that talk with wins in Games 5 and 6.

Then Portland took a commanding lead in Game 7. As the fourth quarter began, the chatter of a Lakers collapse grew louder. The game appeared over for Los Angeles when guard Bonzi Wells connected on a pair of free throws with 10:28 remaining to give the Trail Blazers a 75–60 lead. Then the Trail Blazers' shooting touch went cold.

Bryant and O'Neal earned the starring roles for the Lakers. But during the Game 7 comeback, Brian Shaw stole the spotlight. The reserve guard hit a pair of key three-pointers. And the Trail Blazers kept missing their shots. The collapse was completed in the final minute after the Trail Blazers failed to defend Bryant's lob pass. That set up O'Neal's series-sealing dunk.

"Game 7s are very interesting," Lakers coach Phil Jackson said. "I've never seen any quite like that before."

Portland Trail Blazers guard Damon Stoudamire sits dejected after losing in Game 7 of the 2000 playoffs.

Chapter 4

BIG GOLF CHOKES

Nick Faldo made his putt on the 18th green, clinching the 1996 Masters title. He didn't celebrate. Bending over to pick the ball out of the cup, all he could think of was the player he had just defeated.

Faldo immediately turned to Greg Norman and said, "I don't know what to say. I just want to give you a hug. I feel horrible about what happened. I'm so sorry."

Both men shed tears. Norman had entered the final round with a six-stroke lead over Faldo. In previous tournaments, Norman had developed a reputation for losing final-round leads. But a six-stroke lead appeared safe. At least that was the thought before Norman hooked his first drive into the trees and carded a first-hole bogey.

Nick Faldo, *right*, and Greg Norman walk off the 18th green after the Masters in 1996.

What followed were the four most catastrophic holes of Norman's career. On the ninth hole, Norman's wedge shot fell short of the pin on the hard, downward-slanting green. The ball rolled 30 yards back toward Norman. He could not save par.

On the 10th hole, Norman botched a basic stroke on a simple uphill chip. The ball went 8 feet past the pin. He missed the putt for a bogey. On the 11th hole, Norman struck two ideal shots, setting up a 10-foot birdie putt. It lipped out. The three-foot par putt also stayed out of the hole. Another bogey.

On the 12th hole, a challenging par-3, Faldo placed his tee shot on the putting surface. Norman then pushed his effort to the right and could only watch as the ball rolled into the green-side pond. Norman ended up with a double-bogey.

During the four-hole span, Norman went from a four-stroke lead to a two-stroke deficit. He ended the final round with a 78 and finished five strokes behind Faldo. Of his 20 career Professional Golfers' Association (PGA) victories, Norman claimed two wins in golf's "major" tournaments, both at the British Open. But he never was awarded a green jacket for winning the Masters.

Reckless Van De Velde

In 1999, Jean Van de Velde was playing for the pride of his nation. Walking toward the 18th tee box, Van de Velde held a three-stroke advantage.

Jean Van de Velde looks at his ball in the creek on the 10th hole during the final round at the 1999 British Open.

All Van de Velde had to do was card a double-bogey 6 and he would have become the first Frenchman to win the British Open in 92 years.

He simply played too recklessly at Carnoustie Golf Links. Van de Velde's troubles started when his drive landed in the rough. Instead of playing a safe second shot, he pulled out a 2-iron and went for the green. The shot veered right, slammed off the grandstand railings, struck the top of a brick wall, and bounced back nearly 50 yards. It finally came to rest in knee-high rough. Instead of playing a safe third shot, his swing attempt got caught up in the rough and the shot splashed into a creek.

Van de Velde removed his shoes and socks and waded through ankle-deep water. He looked up and cracked a big smile. He thought about attempting the shot but decided to take a drop.

That strategy didn't work, either. Van de Velde's fifth shot sailed into a bunker.

After all that, Van de Velde was able to collect his emotions. His blast out of the sand landed 6 feet from the hole. He made the putt. Van de Velde's crushing triple-bogey forced a three-way playoff with Paul Lawrie and Justin Leonard. The playoff lasted four holes. Lawrie birdied the final two to earn the victory and complete Van de Velde's collapse, the largest of any major tournament. Lawrie opened the final round 10 strokes behind the leader.

Palmer Provides Drama

Arnold Palmer was one of professional golf's first television stars. It was the 1950s. TV was just beginning to make an impact on society.

Jean Van de Velde smiles as he stands in the water on the 18th hole of the final round at the 1999 British Open.

SNEAD'S ATTENTION SNAPPED

"Slammin' Sammy" Snead was the Tiger Woods of his time. Snead ended his career with 82 wins, the most in tour history. Entering 2013, Woods ranked second with 74. Snead would have won 83 if not for a momentary lapse of focus during the 1947 US Open. Snead was in a playoff duel with Lew Worsham at St. Louis Country Club. On the 18th green, both faced short bids for birdies. Just as Snead was about to putt, Worsham called time out to confirm his opponent's ball was away. Officials finally ruled Snead should putt first. He quickly lined up . . . and missed. Worsham sank his putt for the title.

Jack Nicklaus, Gary Player, and Palmer formed the "Big Three." Curious viewers who tuned in to golf for the first time witnessed a fiery competitor in Palmer. Known as "The King," Palmer had charisma, character, and a reputation for taking daring risks.

Palmer finished his career with 62 PGA victories, including seven majors. From 1958 to 1962, the hall of famer was fitted for four green jackets after capturing the Masters Tournament. For early sports television, Palmer was high drama. And high ratings.

In 1966, golf fans scrambled to black-and-white television sets and tuned in to the US Open. Palmer appeared to be in top form during the front nine. At the turn, Palmer had a commanding seven-stroke lead over Billy Casper.

True to form, Palmer declined to play conservatively. He aimed at breaking the Open's scoring record held then by Ben Hogan.

Arnold Palmer watches as his birdie putt stays out of the cup on the 14th hole in the final round at the 1966 US Open.

SHEEHAN LEARNS A LESSON

Patty Sheehan ran out of patience. During the third round, Sheehan led the 1990 US Women's Open by a commanding 12 strokes. Her apparent victory would have to wait. Rainy weather forced the golfers to suffer through several lengthy delays. Her nerves were racing. Sheehan found it hard to relax. She paced the locker room, hour after hour. The final 36 holes were finally played on the final day. Sheehan was tired. She carded a plus-9 over the final 33 holes. Betsy King ended up winning. Sheehan later said she learned a valuable life lesson. "I learned to eat more nutritious foods," she said, "and get more rest."

Palmer's aggressive play cost him on the par-3 15th hole. He decided not to play a "safe" shot to the middle of the green. Instead Palmer aimed for the pin and landed in a bunker. He settled for a bogey. Meanwhile, Casper was heating up. By the 17th hole they were tied. And they remained tied after 72 holes.

An 18-hole playoff followed the next day. Palmer streaked out to an early advantage. But with eight holes to play, Palmer surrendered a two-stroke lead and finished four strokes behind. Palmer might not have enjoyed all the extra excitement, but the television viewers surely did.

Patty Sheehan reacts to a missed birdie on the seventh hole at the 1990 US Women's Open in Duluth, Georgia.

Chapter 5

BIG INDIVIDUAL CHOKES

All the extra attention he received could have gone to his head. Dan O'Brien was poised to become the toast of the 1992 Olympic Games. As the reigning decathlon world champion, he was a heavy favorite to earn a medal in Barcelona, Spain.

The decathlon is a series of 10 track-and-field events. The Olympic gold medalist in decathlon traditionally is referred to as the "World's Greatest Athlete."

Leading up to the Games, O'Brien was seen and heard everywhere in the media. In the era before the Internet became popular, O'Brien was considered a pop sensation. His on-air advertisements boasted of his ability to sprint 100 meters in 10.3 seconds and whirl a discus 172 feet (52.42 m). He posed for cover photos for countless sports and fitness magazines. He appeared in newspapers and on national and local

US decathlete Dan O'Brien misses his third attempt at his initial height in the pole vault at the 1992 US Olympic Trials.

television sports shows. He was heard on the radio airwaves. Merely qualifying for the Games appeared to be an afterthought to O'Brien and his sponsors.

With so much confidence and pressure to succeed, O'Brien decided against getting "sure points" in the pole vault. He elected to start at the challenging height of 15 feet, 9 inches (4.8 m). He failed to clear the bar three times and registered zero points.

O'Brien fell from first place to twelfth. He could not recover. O'Brien failed to earn enough points to meet the standard for the US Olympic team.

"For half an hour, I walked around with my hands on my head, saying, 'What just happened? Was that really my third attempt?'" O'Brien said. "Somebody had to explain it to me: 'Dude, you're not going to the Olympics.'"

O'Brien rebounded in 1996 to earn a gold medal at the Olympic Games in Atlanta, Georgia.

Trick Trips Up Jacobellis

US women's snowboarder Lindsey Jacobellis cruised down the mountain course in Turin, Italy, seemingly all by herself. Switzerland's Tanja Frieden was in second place and trailed by nearly three seconds. Jacobellis appeared to have clinched the 2006 Olympic Winter Games gold medal in snowboard cross. She was feeling carefree.

At the second-to-last jump the 20-year-old decided to pull off a tricky maneuver. She later said she wanted to add a little more flash to what seemed to be a landslide victory. Jacobellis attempted a backside-method grab. An element of the method grab includes a challenging, 60-degree twist-in from the grandstand. Jacobellis generally did not do tricks during these races. It was a costly decision to do one here. She fell on the landing and slid face-first to the side of the course, covered with snow and frustration.

At the final jump, Frieden flew past Jacobellis. She landed the jump safely—without showboating—and threw both arms up in celebration.

Jacobellis recovered in time to place second. She attempted to explain her in-race decision: "I got caught up in the moment."

Moments after the fall, coach Peter Foley grabbed a camera and examined the move frame-by-frame.

"She definitely styled that a little too hard," Foley said.

Turn 4 Woes

IndyCar Series driver JR Hildebrand is credited with having the best finish for any first-time Indianapolis 500 competitor. He certainly had the most memorable.

The rookie in 2011 found himself in the lead midway through the historic race. He had benefited from a late pit-stop gamble. By extending his fuel, Hildebrand expanded his lead.

MCENROE LOSES FOCUS

John McEnroe was one of the top men's tennis players in the 1980s. Throughout his career, he captured 77 career singles titles, including seven Grand Slam singles titles. McEnroe also was one of the most intense and outspoken players in tennis history. McEnroe entered the 1984 French Open unbeaten. In the final he faced Ivan Lendl. McEnroe easily won the first two sets.

In the third, McEnroe was distracted by a noise from a cameraman. He voiced his displeasure, lost focus, and fell to Lendl in five sets. "Winners know how to handle choking better than losers," McEnroe said.

JR Hildebrand crashes into the wall on the final lap of the 2011 Indianapolis 500 while Dan Wheldon cruises by en route to victory.

On the final turn of the final lap, Hildebrand was free of traffic. He was certain to win. Then he suddenly lost control of his car. It smashed into the outside wall of Turn 4. After the crash, Hildebrand was able to straighten out the damaged car. He ended up placing second to two-time champion Dan Wheldon.

Hildebrand later compared his gaffe with that of baseball's Bill Buckner. The Boston Red Sox first baseman is remembered most for his error in Game 6 of the 1986 World Series. Buckner's misplay of a slow grounder allowed the New York Mets to score the winning run. The Mets went on to win Game 7.

"I feel for Buckner every time I see that [replay]," Hildebrand said.

Chapter 6

BIG HOCKEY CHOKES

A record National Hockey League (NHL) crowd of more than 16,000 fans filled Maple Leaf Gardens in Toronto. They came anticipating a chance to witness history during Game 7 of the 1942 Stanley Cup finals. Never before had a team rallied from a 3–0 series deficit to claim the Cup.

Just a few days earlier a Detroit Red Wings championship appeared inevitable. The Red Wings had cruised to wins in the series' first three games over the Toronto Maple Leafs. Then Toronto came back to win the next three. The result was Game 7 back at Maple Leaf Gardens.

Game 7 began before a sold-out crowd of screaming fans. The Red Wings opened the scoring in the second period on a goal by Syd Howe. The Red Wings maintained that one-goal lead at the seven-minute mark of the third period.

Syd Howe was a legend for the Detroit Red Wings, but he couldn't lead his team to the 1942 Stanley Cup.

Then Sweeney Schriner scored to tie the game for Toronto. The Maple Leafs clinched the Cup with two late goals. The record crowd did indeed see history. Along with the Red Wings, the 1975 Pittsburgh Penguins and the 2010 Boston Bruins were the only teams in NHL history to lose a playoff series after winning the first three games through 2012.

Miracle and a Mistake

Coach Viktor Tikhonov is one of the Soviet Union's all-time greatest coaches. There was one decision, however, he would like to take back.

Tikhonov acknowledged his worst coaching move came in the famous loss to Team USA during the 1980 Olympic Winter Games in Lake Placid, New York. The Soviets came into the tournament as heavy favorites. And backstopping the team was goalie Vladislav Tretiak. He was considered the best goalie in the world at the time.

However, things began to go awry in the medal-round game against underdog Team USA. Late in the first period, Tretiak allowed a long

Vladislav Tretiak of the Soviet Union was considered the world's best goalie going into the 1980 Olympic Winter Games.

rebound to slide in the direction of Mark Johnson. The American forward collected the puck and drove to the net. He scored with one second remaining in the period, tying the game at 2–2.

Upset, Tikhonov benched Tretiak. Tretiak's replacement, Vladimir Myshkin, gave up two third-period goals and lost his balance on Team USA's "Miracle" goal by captain Mike Eruzione. The Soviets lost, 4–3.

The Soviet Union had a roster stocked with professionals. But the team was denied a chance to win a gold medal by a collection of US college players and amateurs in the "Miracle on Ice."

The Wrong Side of Another Miracle

When hockey fans think of the Edmonton Oilers of the 1980s, they generally think of three things: Wayne Gretzky's offensive magic, four Stanley Cups from 1984 to 1988, and a loaded roster of six future hall of famers.

The Oilers were an NHL dynasty through much of the decade. They were one of the league's highest scoring teams *and* one of the top defensive clubs.

Before earning their first Cup, though, the maturing powerhouse endured some growing pains. For the 1982 playoffs, the Oilers earned home-ice advantage by placing first in the Campbell Conference by a 17-point margin. The Oilers' first-round opponent was the Los Angeles Kings, who barely qualified.

Brian Propp (16) of the Minnesota North Stars shoots on Chicago Blackhawks goalie Ed Belfour during the 1991 playoffs.

BRUINS COME UP DRY

The 1970–71 Boston Bruins had everything going for them. They placed first in the East Division with 121 points. They paced the 14-team league in goals scored (399) and ranked third in goals allowed (207). The Bruins were loaded with superstars such as Bobby Orr, Phil Esposito, Johnny Bucyk, and Ken Hodge. And they were facing an unknown goalie in the first round of the playoffs. Soon everyone would know Montreal Canadiens goalie Ken Dryden. The future hall of famer stood up to his first playoff challenge. Dryden forced a Game 7 and the Bruins did not have an answer in a 4–2 loss.

The five-game series was tied after two games. Then, in the third game, the Oilers surrendered a five-goal lead and lost in overtime. The game became known as "The Miracle on Manchester." It was named after the street on which the arena was located. Edmonton eventually lost in five games.

The young Oilers appeared to learn from the setback. The team qualified for its first Stanley Cup finals the next season and in 1984 captured its first Cup.

The Oilers were not immune to setbacks, though. Their quest for a third consecutive Stanley Cup championship came to an end in Game 7 of the 1986 Smythe Division final. The score was tied at 2–2 against the Calgary Flames. Oilers defenseman Steve Smith skated to the boards behind his team's net. Smith retrieved a puck and attempted to execute a breakout.

But Smith's pass ricocheted off Oilers goalie Grant Fuhr's skate and slid into his own net at 14:46 of the third period. Calgary was now up 3–2.

On his twenty-third birthday, Smith gave a big gift to Perry Berezan. The Calgary forward was credited with the series-clinching goal for being the closest Flames skater to the play.

FUN FACTS

★ Brazil's victory medals were already engraved with the players' names. Victory speeches by World Cup organizers and politicians were written and rehearsed. The decisive 1950 World Cup match against underdog Uruguay nearly brought the host country of Brazil to a standstill. Brazilians expected to celebrate a championship. Few expected Uruguay's defense to handle and confuse Brazil's attacking offense the way it did. Brazil finally scored early in the second half. But Uruguay answered with two goals to win 2–1. When the match ended, stunned Brazilian fans sat in silence.

★ Perhaps no sport has featured as many chokes as golf. European golfer Bernhard Langer missed a 6-foot par putt that would have clinched his match and the 1991 Ryder Cup. Golfer Scott Hoch was 2 feet from claiming the 1989 Masters. On the first playoff hole, Hoch missed the tap-in putt. Hoch lost to Nick Faldo on the next playoff hole. Rory McIlroy held a four-stroke lead at the 2011 Masters entering the final round. He carded an 80. Through 2013, it was the worst round by any Masters third-round leader.

★ In a 1980 welterweight title fight rematch, Roberto Duran endured a hard right uppercut from Sugar Ray Leonard. Duran turned to the referee and uttered, "*No mas*," which is Spanish for "no more." He did not want to fight any more.

★ During a 1927 Wimbledon semifinal match, Bill Tilden led 6–2, 6–2, 5–1 (30–0). Despite being just two points from winning, he ended up losing the game, the set, and eventually the match.

GLOSSARY

AWAY

In golf, the person whose ball is farthest from the hole.

CHARISMA

An attractiveness that can inspire others.

CONTENTION

In the hunt.

CUTTER

A cut fastball that displays late lateral movement. Its rotation is like a slider but with the speed of a fastball.

DYNASTY

A team that wins many championships over a short period of time.

ERROR

A misplayed ball by a fielder in a baseball game that results in a base runner advancing.

LAPSE

A momentary decline of concentration or performance.

LORE

Information that gets passed down through the ages.

MOMENTUM

A continued strong performance based on recent successes.

PENNANT

A flag. In baseball, it symbolizes that a team won its league championship.

PLAYOFFS

A series of games or matches to determine a champion.

ROOKIE

A first-year player in a new league.

UNDERDOG

A team or athlete that is predicted to lose in an upcoming game or match.

FOR MORE INFORMATION

Selected Bibliography

Editors at ESPN. *ESPN College Basketball Encyclopedia: The Complete History of the Men's Game*. New York: Ballantine Books and ESPN Books, 2009.

Jenkins, Dan. *Jenkins at the Majors: Sixty Years of the World's Best Golf Writing, from Hogan to Tiger*. New York: Doubleday, 2009.

Kennedy, Kostya, ed. *The Hockey Book*. New York: Sports Illustrated Books, 2010.

MacCambridge, Michael. *ESPN College Football Encyclopedia*. New York: ESPN, 2005.

McGinn, Bob. *The Ultimate Super Bowl Book: A Complete Reference to the Stats, Stars and Stories Behind Football's Biggest Game – and Why the Best Team Won*. Minneapolis, MN: MVP Books, 2012.

Sowell, David. *The Masters: A Hole-by-Hole History of America's Golf Classic (Second Edition)*. Washington DC: Brassey's, Inc., 2003.

Further Readings

Berman, Len. *The Greatest Moments in Sports: Upsets and Underdogs*. Naperville, IL: Sourcebooks, 2012.

Christopher, Matt. *Great Moments in the Summer Olympics*. New York: Little, Brown and Co., 2012.

Lupica, Mike. *Shoot-out: A Comeback Kids Novel*. New York: Philomel Books, 2010.

Martirano, Ron. *Book of Football Stuff: Great Records, Weird Happenings, Odd Facts, Amazing Moments and Cool Things*. New York: Imagine Publications, 2009.

McGinn, Bob. *Sports in American Life: A History*. Reno, NV: Wiley-Blackwell, 2012.

Web Links

To learn more about the biggest chokes in sports, visit ABDO Publishing Company online at **www.abdopublishing.com**. Web sites about the biggest chokes in sports are featured on our Book Links page. These links are routinely monitored and updated to provide the most current information available.

Places to Visit

Naismith Memorial Basketball Hall of Fame
1000 Hall Fame Ave
Springfield, MA 01105
(413) 781-6500
www.hoophall.com
The Naismith Memorial Basketball Hall of Fame honors basketball's greatest players and moments.

National Baseball Hall of Fame and Museum
25 Main Street
Cooperstown, NY 13326
(888) 425-5633
www.baseballhall.org
This hall of fame and museum highlights the greatest players and moments in the history of baseball.

Pro Football Hall of Fame
2121 George Halas Drive NW
Canton, OH 44708
(330) 456-8207
www.profootballhof.com
This hall of fame and museum highlights the greatest players and moments in the history of the NFL.

INDEX

About the Author

Jeff Hawkins was an award-winning sportswriter for parts of four decades. Career highlights include covering the NFL's Carolina Panthers (2011) and NHL's Chicago Blackhawks (2003–06). Hawkins captured two national Associated Press Sports Editors awards and six regional/state honors for feature writing. Hawkins resides in North Carolina with his wife and young son.